Prelude to the Holocaust

Jane Shuter

Heinemann Library
Chicago, Illinois

Designed by Joanna Sapwell and Tinstar Design
Illustrations by Martin Griffin
Originated by Ambassador Litho Ltd
Printed in Hong Kong, by Wing King Tong

07 06 05 04 03
10 9 8 7 6 5 4 3 2 1

Library of Congress
Cataloging-in-Publication Data
Shuter, Jane.
  Prelude to the Holocaust / Jane Shuter.
    p. cm. -- (The Holocaust)
Includes index.
Summary: Offers an account of the events leading up to
the Holocaust and
the early days of that period of persecution.
  ISBN 1-4034-0813-0 (HC), 1-4034-3205-8 (Pbk.)
  1. Holocaust, Jewish (1939-1945)--Juvenile literature. 2.
Jews--Persecutions--Juvenile literature. 3.
Germany--History--1933-1945--Juvenile literature. 4.
Germany--Ethnic
relations--Juvenile literature. [1. Holocaust, Jewish (1939-
1945) 2.
Jews--Persecutions--Germany. 3. Germany--History--1933-
1945.] I. Title.
II. Holocaust (Chicago, Ill.)
  D804.34 .S73 2002
  940.53'18--dc21   2002006850

Acknowledgments
The author and publisher are grateful to the following for
permission to reproduce copyright material: pp. 5 (top), 5
(bottom), 37 Emma Robertson & Magnet Harlequin; pp. 6,
7, 13, 16, 20, 24, 29, 44 USHMM; p. 9 Corbis; pp. 11, 12
Mary Evans picture library; p. 13 Sterling Memorial
Library, Yale University; pp. 14, 47 AKG; pp. 15, 39
Auschwitz-Birkenau State Museum; p. 17 Robert Hunt
Library (& Mary Evans Reserve); p. 18 Anne Frank
Stichting; pp. 19, 26, 27, 33, 40 Bildarchiv Preussisher
Kulturbesitz; pp. 23, 45 Hulton Archive; p. 28
Bundesarchive; p. 30 Ullstein Bild; p. 31 Tomi Ungerer &
Diogenes Verlag AG Zurich; p. 32 Imperial War Museum;
p. 35 Hessisches Hauptstaatsarchiv in Wiesbaden; pp. 36,
38, 42 Yad Vashem; p. 41 Rudolf Vrba; p. 43 Magnum; pp.
46, 49 Associated Press; p. 48 Jewish Chronicle; p. 49 Kurt
Fuchel.

Cover photograph of Adolf Hitler surveying a mass
gathering of Nazis, reproduced with permission of
Popperfoto.

Special thanks to Ronald Smelser and Sally Brown-Winter.

About the series consultants
Ronald Smelser is a history professor at the University
of Utah. He has written or edited eight books on the
Holocaust and over three dozen articles. His recent
publications include *Learning About the Holocaust: A Student
Guide* (4 vol.) and *Lessons and Legacies: The Holocaust and
Justice*. Professor Smelser is also a past president of the
German Studies Association.

Sally Brown-Winter has worked in the field of Jewish
Education as a principal and teacher for over 25 years.
In her schools, the Shoah—its history, lessons, and
implications—have been explored from kindergarten
through high school.

Every effort has been made to contact copyright holders of
any material reproduced in this book. Any omissions will
be rectified in subsequent printings if notice is given to the
publisher.

Some words are shown in bold, **like this.** You can find out what they mean by looking
in the glossary.

Contents

What Was the Holocaust?

In ancient times, the word **holocaust** meant "an offering to the gods that was completely burned away." By medieval times it was used to mean, "a huge destruction or sacrifice." Today, the Holocaust refers to the deliberate attempt by the **Nazi** government of Germany to destroy all of the **Jewish** people in their power. The word was first used in this way in the 1950s.

When Did the Holocaust Take Place?

The Holocaust happened before and during World War II (1939–1945). However, Jewish people were persecuted and killed from the moment the Nazis came to power in 1933. World War II helped the Nazis cover up and excuse mass killings.

Historians have tried hard to determine how many people died in the Holocaust. Their work suggests that around six million Jews were murdered. The scale of the killing was such that a new word was invented to describe it—genocide. Rafael Lemkin, a Jewish lawyer living in the United States, first used this word in 1943 to describe the wiping out of a whole **race,** that is, a group of people with the same **ancestors.** While "the Holocaust" mostly refers to the Nazi killings, "genocide" is used to describe any attempt to murder all members of a racial group.

Survivors

In many cases, only one or two members of a family survived the Holocaust. In this photograph of the Zylberberg family, only the baby on the right, Perec, survived. His sister, Esther, who was born after the photo was taken, also survived. Another survivor, Norbert Wollheim, said:

All the others who had gone with me to Auschwitz or had been taken there at other times, would never return. My wife, my child, my parents, and about 70 other relations: uncles, aunts, cousins, all gone.

Possessions

These are just a very few of the possessions on display in the museum at Auschwitz in Poland. They show that the Nazis killed men and women, young and old. These items were found in the Auschwitz-Birkenau camp. There were 30 warehouses, crammed full. The Nazis tried to destroy these warehouses and the **gas chambers,** when they heard that the advancing Russian soldiers were close to the camp. But it was too late to destroy everything.

Were There Other Victims of the Holocaust?

The Holocaust swept up non-Jewish victims, too. These included other peoples, such as Gypsies and Poles, that the Nazis saw as separate, "inferior" races. The Nazis had definite, unreasonable ideas about race. People who did not fit the Nazi ideas about a perfect society—including the physically and mentally disabled, homosexuals, and political opponents of the Nazis—were also victims.

How Do We Know?

- One of the most important sources of information about the Holocaust is the memories of people who survived it.
- Many people who did not survive the Holocaust kept diaries and collected photographs and other evidence. Some of them managed to hide this evidence, or leave it with friends, so it has survived to be used as evidence today.
- The Nazis kept detailed records, documents that show what went on during the Holocaust. When they realized that the **Allies** were winning the war, the Nazis tried to destroy the evidence of their worst crimes. They only partly succeeded; a great deal of evidence survived.
- A few places that were used in the Holocaust are still standing. Terezín in the Czech Republic was used as a **ghetto,** where Jews were shut in and forced to live away from other communities. The Auschwitz-Birkenau **concentration** and **death camp,** in Poland, has also survived.
- In 1945–1946, many Nazis were tried at Nuremberg, Germany. The lawyers at the trials produced evidence from survivors, from members of the **SS,** and from people who had worked for the SS in various camps.
- The Allied soldiers who **liberated** the camps recorded what the camps were like in words, on film, and in pictures.

The Jewish People

Jews see themselves as a people with common **ancestors** who can be traced back to Biblical times. They are united by their religion, Judaism; by a common language of prayer, Hebrew; and by a strong culture. These things bind Jewish people together, but have also made it easy for others to identify and isolate them.

Judaism

The religion of the Jewish people is Judaism. It teaches that there is one God, who has chosen the Jewish people to be special. God will look after them, but in return, they have to live life according to His commands. Jewish people follow the teachings of their holy writings—the Torah. These writings were recorded on scrolls, written in different lands at different times.

The Torah is made up of the Five Books of Moses that are also the first five books of the Old Testament of the Christian Bible. Other writings also overlap with books in the Christian Old Testament. The scrolls record the teachings of prophets, later teachings, and stories that were passed down orally at first and written down later. The Torah covers all aspects of life. It gives instructions about diet, dress, and manners. It also gives religious instructions. For example, Jews are expected to pray at home, as well as in synagogues (places of communal worship), so religion and everyday life are tightly bound together. The Torah is written in Hebrew, the language that unites all Jewish people, no matter where they live.

Family Celebrations

Family worship is as important as worship in synagogues for Jewish people. Each week on the Sabbath, families light candles, drink wine, eat special bread called challah, and thank God for His blessings. Holy days are also celebrated in the home. This Polish Jewish family, photographed in Lodz in the early 1930s, is celebrating the Passover festival.

Dietary Customs

The Torah has rules about the kinds of food that Jewish people can eat and how it should be prepared. Jews can only eat certain kinds of meat. For instance, they cannot eat pigs or rabbits. The meat they do eat has to be prepared by butchers in a particular way. The need to buy the right kind of meat, butter, bread, and other foodstuffs was one reason Jewish people chose to live together. This photo of a Jewish butcher's shop was taken in Danzig, Poland, in the 1930s.

A Sense of Community

The Torah tells Jewish people to take care of others, especially the poor and the sick. It also values education. Children are taught to read Hebrew at an early age so that they will be able to read the Torah. Jewish communities set up their own hospitals, schools, and other institutions to care for the old, sick, and orphaned.

Flung Across the World

Historians tell how, in New Testament times, the Jews were thrown out of the Holy Land, their land in parts of modern-day Israel, Syria, and Lebanon. Jewish people have moved around the world, settling in a place sometimes for many generations.

They see themselves as both Jewish and belonging to the country that they have settled in. The Torah tells people to "seek the peace" of the place where they are living and to pray for it.

Differences in Faith

While Jewish people share many values and beliefs, they have not always agreed about how to live. Mostly, Jewish people have argued over how strictly they should follow the rules in the Torah. Some Jews say the Torah is the exact word of God. They believe is must be obeyed in every way and cannot be changed. Other Jews believe that the Torah is the word of God as interpreted by people. They believe that some of the commands in the Torah, while right for some generations, can become irrelevant. They think people have a right to choose how they follow some of the rules.

Anti-Semitism

The **Nazis** were anti-Semitic. **Anti-Semitism** is the hatred or unfair treatment of **Jewish** people. Although the term was first used in 1879, anti-Semitism has been around for thousands of years. The Book of Exodus, part of the Christian Bible and the Jewish Torah, tells how the Egyptian pharaohs persecuted the Jewish people.

Was Anti-Semitism Constant?

Anti-Semitism was not constant anywhere. It flared up in different countries for different reasons at different times. However, many Jewish communities have existed in the same places for hundreds of years without experiencing anti-Semitism. For instance, between about 500 C.E. and 1000 C.E. there are very few recorded instances of anti-Semitism in Europe. After 1000, there was a long period of persecution in Europe that died down by about 1600.

This persecution varied in intensity. Some parts of Europe were unaffected, especially remote agricultural areas.

Why Were Jewish People Persecuted?

Jews were persecuted for different religious and social reasons.

- *Religious reasons:* Christians blamed the Jews for crucifying Jesus Christ. Also, very few Jews were prepared to change their religion and become Christian. For this reason, they attracted hostility from Christians that could flare up into expulsions, persecution, and murder.
- *Social reasons:* Jews were often seen as strangers no matter how they tried to fit into the countries they lived in. Their language, faith, and culture made them different. When danger or disaster struck, Jews were an easy target for blame. They were blamed for economic problems, epidemics of disease, and even natural disasters like floods.

Burning Jews

This medieval engraving shows Jews being burned during an outbreak of persecution in Germany in the Middle Ages.

The First Ghetto

The first Jewish ghetto was set up in Venice, Italy, in 1516. All Jews had to move to one of the smaller islands. Christian soldiers guarded the only two bridges off the island. Space was limited, and as the number of people grew, the buildings were made taller. Jews were allowed to leave the ghetto in the daytime, but they had to wear special hats and badges so that people would know they were Jewish. The jobs they were allowed to do were also limited.

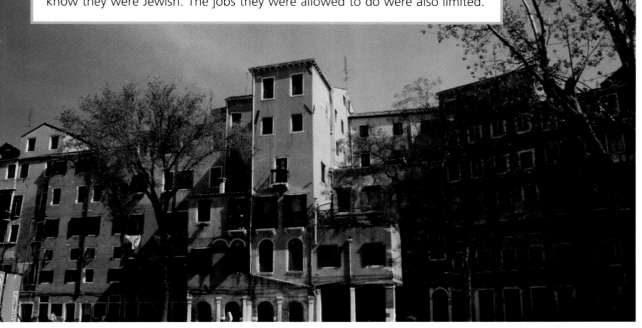

Persecuting Jewish People

There were a variety of ways in which people persecuted the Jews. The Nazis used all of these when they came to power.

- They made Jews live in **ghettos**—separate areas within a city. When countries set up ghettos, Jews were forced to live in them and could not live anywhere else. This was very different from Jews choosing to live together to be near synagogues, schools, and stores.
- Between about 1000 and 1700, many European countries also passed laws that said Jews had to wear special clothing so they could be recognized easily.
- Some countries expelled the Jews who lived there; this happened in England in 1290 and in Spain in 1492. When the Jews were expelled from a country, they all had to leave within a certain number of days, leaving many of their possessions behind. If they had not left by that time, they would be forced out or killed.
- Sometimes anti-Semitic feelings in an area or country grew so strong that people hunted down Jews and killed them. Generally, this happened in only some parts of a country. For example, in 1106 the people of York, England, killed 150 English Jews. It could also happen throughout a country, as happened in Russia. Over 100,000 Jews were killed in Russia between 1648 and 1656.

Hitler and the Nazi Party

The **Nazi** Party, led by Adolf Hitler, legally came to power in Germany in 1933. They had not always carefully obeyed the law, and used the freedoms of a democratic society to overthrow it.

Adolf Hitler

Adolf Hitler was born in Austria in 1889. He did poorly in school and then went to Vienna, hoping to be accepted as an art student. He was told he did not have enough talent. Hitler then spent five years living in poverty in Vienna, trying to earn a living by painting and selling postcards. It was at this time, he said later, that he began to hate educated people, **Communists,** and **Jews.** He began to think that they were in a conspiracy to keep him from the success he thought he should have.

In 1914, Hitler joined the German army and fought in World War I (1914–1918). He was awarded several medals for bravery. Germany's surrender in 1918, and the harsh Treaty of Versailles that ended the war, upset him. He linked Germany's defeat to alleged Jewish treachery.

Many people, even those who had fought Germany, felt the Treaty was too harsh. Hitler thought that the German government had been wrong to sign the Treaty of Versailles. He decided he would go into politics and lead Germany to a wonderful future.

The Treaty of Versailles

- The Treaty took away all of the land Germany had gained during the war.
- It took away some of Germany's richest land in Europe and all of its colonies abroad.
- It made Germany officially take the blame for causing the war. This had not happened in a peace treaty before.
- It ordered Germany to pay for repairs in countries that were badly damaged by the war.
- It forced Germany to reduce the size of its armed forces drastically.

Territory lost by Germany to other countries

Territory lost by Germany to the League of Nations

Area formerly Austria-Hungary

Territory lost by Russia

Demilitarized zone

"One Leader"

From the beginning, Hitler made sure his picture was everywhere. Christabel Bielenberg, an Englishwoman living in Berlin, had a landlady whose son collected cards like this one. She remembers:

> Hans believed that he had found the solution to all Germany's problems. Over cups of cocoa, with picture postcards of Hitler in many different poses on the walls around us, he told me why the Nazis were the only party that could save Germany from complete chaos. One of their slogans was "One leader, one nation, one people."

Going into Politics

Many other Germans felt betrayed by Germany's surrender. Several political parties sprang up to oppose the government that signed the Treaty of Versailles. In 1919, Hitler joined one of these—the German Workers' Party. Hitler agreed with its aims and thought it was small enough for him to take it over.

By 1920, Hitler was one of the small group that drew up the Twenty-Five Points, the program that outlined the aims of the Party. By 1921 he was its leader and had renamed the party the *Nationalsozialistiche Deutsche Arbeiterpartei*: the National Socialist German Workers' Party, or Nazis for short. The Nazis stressed their support for "the workers" against people in Germany who were "exploiting" them. They argued that ordinary people needed work and food, which the Nazis would provide if they ran Germany. They said that the existing government could do this, but instead it chose to plot against the German people with Jews, Marxists, Communists, the rich, and "intellectuals."

Nazi Aims

Nazi Party aims included the following:
- scrapping the Treaty of Versailles;
- gaining land in which to settle all German-speaking people;
- taking control of even more land for these people to expand into;
- ensuring only people of German blood could be German **citizens**—this automatically excluded Jews;
- allowing only German citizens to have rights in German lands;
- giving complete power to the state (government), which should use it to care for German citizens;
- requiring that non-German citizens leave German lands; and
- requiring that German citizens put the interest of the national community before their own.

The Nazi State

Hitler was sent to prison after the **Nazis** attempted to take over in Bavaria. While there, he wrote a book called *Mein Kampf* (My Struggle), outlining his aims for the Nazi Party. These expanded the Twenty-Five Points, aiming to create a German **Reich** with a single leader—Hitler. One of the first things the new Nazi state would do was to retake the land Germany lost in the Treaty of Versailles. It would then take more land. The German people needed more room to expand into. This idea of "living space," or *Lebensraum*, was important to the Nazis and was used to justify their expansion across Europe. In *Mein Kampf* Hitler wrote:

> There are huge areas of unused land waiting to be used. Nature has not set this land aside for any particular nation or **race**—it belongs to those with the strength to take it. A state has a duty to make sure that its people have enough Lebensraum.

Hitler's New Plan

Hitler had tried to take over the German government by force and had failed. So, in a letter sent to one of his followers while he was in prison, Hitler outlined a new plan:

> Instead of gaining power by armed revolt, we will have to enter the Reichstag [German parliament] *and win seats from Catholics and Marxists. Outvoting them may take longer than outshooting them, but we will win a majority and then—Germany.*

Storm Troopers

As soon as he became leader of the Nazis, Hitler set up a private army of "storm troopers" **(SA)**. The SA were regularly involved in fighting, usually with opposing political groups, to try to stop them from campaigning against the Nazis. At first, Hitler hoped to use the SA to take over Germany by force. In 1923, the Nazis tried this in Munich, Bavaria. They tried to take over the Bavarian government, intending then to march on Berlin. The plot was crushed by the Bavarian state police.

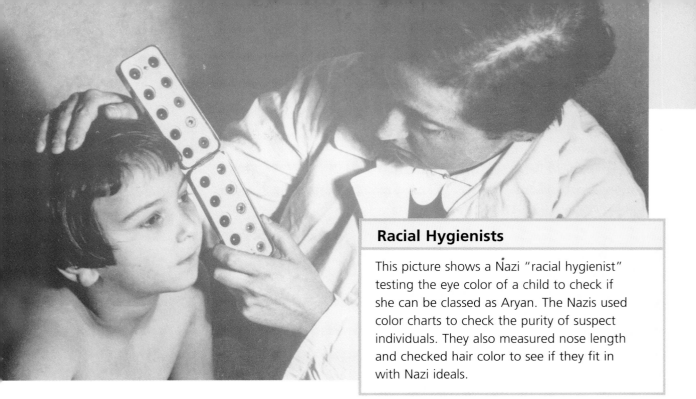

Racial Superiority

From about 1500, European explorers came across groups of people who did not look like them or behave like them. Differences in behavior were thought to be mainly caused by physical differences, which were explained by different **ancestors.** Thus, Europeans divided people into different racial groups, depending on their ancestry. They wrongly assumed that Europeans were superior. In 1835, a Frenchman set out levels of superiority among white Europeans. He said: "I believe that the **Aryan** race—white Europeans of the blonde, Nordic type—are superior." The Nazis took this idea of superior Aryans and added the idea that these people all had "pure German blood." This idea made the nonsense worse. The idea that Aryans were superior, however, was useful to the Nazis. It allowed them to excuse any mistreatment of non-Aryans.

Racial Purity

The Nazi idea about a superior Aryan race that had "pure German blood" was untrue, but Nazi scientists invented proof for it. It became one of the Nazis most important beliefs. Hitler wrote in *Mein Kampf*: "No boy or girl must leave school without having a clear understanding of racial purity and the importance of keeping the racial blood pure."

The Nazis also believed that German citizens should be healthy. The "unfit"—physically or mentally disabled people and **asocials,** such as beggars and drunks—should be weeded out. They, like non-Aryans, could pollute pure German blood. Ideas about social groups were being discussed in other countries, too. In 1910, the English politician Winston Churchill suggested that about 100,000 "degenerate" British people should have medical operations to keep them from having children, or they should be shut away.

Nazi Rallies

While Hitler was in prison, the **Nazi** Party collapsed. As soon as he was released in 1924, Hitler set up the Nazi Party again and began working to take over Germany by winning votes in elections. He was a good speaker, so he made sure that the Nazi campaign had a lot of big meetings, called rallies, at which he spoke. In that way, he spread his ideas to as many people as possible.

Hitler's Speeches

Hitler's speeches all followed a carefully calculated pattern. They began with the history of Germany and the Nazi Party. Then came some information, such as a government decision to introduce **rationing.** The reasons were given mixed with angry accusations against people, such as **Communists** or **Jews,** that Hitler wanted Germans to hate. The speeches ended with Hitler telling the audience he would work hard to make Germany glorious and so must they. Hitler had a series of photos taken of himself making dramatic gestures so he could decide which were the most effective ones to use in speechmaking. Stefan Lorant, a Hungarian journalist in Berlin in the 1930s, described the effect of Hitler's speeches:

> *The audience was hypnotized. It shouted with joy; it yelled; it wept. The meeting had nothing to do with politics anymore. It had become a mass of believers in miracles.*

Propaganda

Hitler was very aware of the power of **propaganda.** Propaganda is information and ideas that are worded and presented so that people will accept and believe them, even if they are not true. Starting in 1924, the Nazis used posters, radio broadcasts, leaflets, rallies, and demonstrations to spread their propaganda. They kept each message simple and repeated it over and over again. They used words such as "we" and "our" that suggested that the Nazis were on the same side as the voters. They used violence against other political parties and propaganda that stressed the rises in unemployment and cost of living under the government of the time. As a result, Hitler and the Nazis won 230 of the 615 seats in the *Reichstag* in the July 1932 election.

The Nazis in Power

Once the Nazis came to power, they began making sure they stayed there. In July 1933, they banned all other political parties. They set up the **Third Reich** led by the *Führer,* Adolf Hitler. They began to wipe out all opposition. They set up **concentration camps**—prisons where anyone could be sent, without trial, for being "a danger to the nation." Most camp prisoners in the early 1930s were political opponents, especially Communists. The Nazis saw Communists as dangerous because they had very different beliefs from the Nazis and because they had also been gaining support in Germany. They were, in some ways, the biggest political threat to the Nazis.

Later, these concentration camps were used for people arrested on **racial** grounds—Poles, Russians, and Jews.

An Obedient Nation

The Nazis had always said that no single person's rights were more important than the "good" of Germany. They, of course, were convinced that they knew what was good for Germany. Their view was that to make Germany great they needed obedient **citizens.** They expected "good Germans" to put Germany first and to obey the Nazis. For example, good Germans should accept low wages, report a family member who was disloyal to the Nazis, or report a neighbor who was a Communist.

Jews in Germany in the 1930s

When the **Nazis** came to power in 1933, there were about 503,000 **Jewish** people in Germany. This number came to less than one out of every hundred people, yet the Nazis were saying that Germany was overrun with Jews. Many of them had been born in Germany, as had their parents and grandparents. They saw themselves as German. Many of their non-Jewish neighbors did, too. Many German Jews did not live or work separately from other Germans; they were part of the same community. Some Jews married non-Jews, either giving up their Jewish faith entirely or converting to the religion of their partner.

German Businesses

Many German Jews ran their own small businesses, carefully built up over many years. As well as having their emotional roots, family, and friends in Germany, they had all their savings tied up in Germany, too. They did not want to leave. Many believed Hitler was not against ordinary Jews who lived quietly. Bertha Leverton, a Jewish girl living in Munich, remembers:

> *Unfortunately my parents thought: "The Nazis don't mean us. They just mean the rich Jews with the big firms and big, big businesses. We'll stay put. It'll all blow over."*

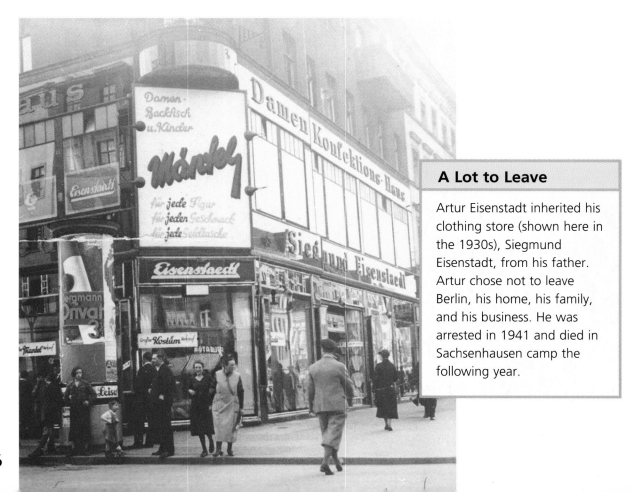

A Lot to Leave

Artur Eisenstadt inherited his clothing store (shown here in the 1930s), Siegmund Eisenstadt, from his father. Artur chose not to leave Berlin, his home, his family, and his business. He was arrested in 1941 and died in Sachsenhausen camp the following year.

Anti-Semitism in Action

As soon as they came to power, the Nazis began to put their **racial** theories into practice. They increased anti-Jewish **propaganda.** Nazi groups, such as the **Hitler Youth** and the **SA,** used violence against Jews and encouraged all non-Jewish people to do this, too. The Nazis heaped as many "sins" as they could invent on the heads of the Jewish people. They said that Jews had "bad" blood, were **Communists,** caused Germany to lose World War I, and were making money at the expense of the German people. By the late 1930s, Nazi accusations were wilder. The Nazis claimed that Jews regularly murdered Germans, they even sacrificed non-Jewish children in their religious ceremonies.

Legal Persecution

The Nazis passed laws against the Jews, making it increasingly difficult for Jews to live in Germany. On April 7, 1933, Jewish government workers, including civil servants and teachers, lost their jobs.

Next, Jews were banned from sports, "cultural activities," and journalism. They could not join the army or go to college. Rules were made to make life difficult and humiliating for Jews. They had to use separate park benches and public transportation. They could not use public swimming pools, keep pets, or use "Jewish names" in telegrams.

The Nuremberg Laws

As laws were enforced against Jews, it became clear that no one was sure what made a person legally Jewish. In 1935, the Nuremberg Laws declared what made a person Jewish in Nazi law: anyone with three Jewish grandparents, or two Jewish grandparents who followed the Jewish faith was Jewish, even if they did not follow the Jewish faith themselves. To the Nazis it was **ancestry,** not religion, that made a person Jewish. The Nuremberg Laws also said that Jews could not be German **citizens,** marry non-Jews, or employ anyone under the age of 45 who was of "German blood."

17

Leaving Germany

Getting Out Early

It was hard for some **Jewish** people to decide to leave Germany. Even so, people did leave. The Franks, a Jewish family living in Frankfurt, had considered leaving in 1932. They waited because, as Otto Frank explained:

> *When we heard the **SA** singing songs like "When Jewish blood splatters off the knife . . ." we talked of leaving. But there was the question: How will you support yourself if you go away and give up almost everything?*

They were able to leave in 1933 because Edith Frank's brother helped Otto to set up a business in Amsterdam, in the Netherlands.

By 1936, about 78,000 Jewish people, roughly one in six of the Jewish population in Germany in 1933, had left. Those who left usually had the fewest ties to Germany and had enough money to start life again somewhere else. Many of them went to nearby European countries, such as France and the Netherlands.

Anne Frank

Once out of Germany, people settled down to build a new life in their new country. They could relax, and even enjoy themselves. They had no way of knowing that the German army would march into country after country in mainland Europe. They thought they were safe. In the Netherlands, Otto and Edith Frank's two daughters, Anne and Margot, went to local schools in Amsterdam, learned Dutch, and made lots of friends. This picture shows Anne, circled at the back, with her classmates at school.

Where to Go?

People often, but not always, moved to countries where they already had family or friends. Families or friends could help with immigration paperwork and finding jobs. The new immigrants could stay with friends or family and meet new people through them. All of this made it easier to settle. There were other things to think about when deciding where to go, though. Most Jewish **refugees** went to other European countries. These countries were easier and cheaper to get to and many people felt it would be easier to settle into another country in Europe.

Some refugees wanted to leave Europe altogether. Many wanted to go to the United States. They had to have a visa, though, and the U.S. gave out only a set number of visas to each country per year. Another destination was Palestine, which had been controlled by the British since 1917.

Nazi Policy

In the early 1930s, **Nazi** policy about Jewish emigration was not clear. Herman Goering, the Nazi in charge of Jewish emigration, had ordered that Jews should be encouraged to emigrate "by all available means." However, the Nazis heavily taxed those who were leaving, making it harder for them to take anything valuable out of the country. Many lost the bulk of their wealth on leaving. This loss made it more difficult to start a new life, so fewer wanted to go.

In 1936, during the Olympic Games, when there were many more foreigners in Germany than usual, the Nazis were much less brutal to Jewish people. Some refugees even believed that the worst was over and returned to Germany. Many people left the decision to leave until it was too late. Beginning in 1938, it became increasingly difficult to leave the country.

19

Quotas

During the 1930s, many countries had economic problems—unemployment, hunger, and homelessness. Governments did not want to add to these problems by taking in large numbers of immigrants from other countries. The U.S. had a quota system—only a set number of people could immigrate each year. Most other countries also had immigration laws of some kind.

The Evian Conference

In July 1938, in the French town of Evian, 32 governments sent representatives to a meeting organized by the United States to discuss the **refugees.** By this time most countries had a quota system. Their main concern was not to increase their economic and social problems. They made few allowances for the desperate situation of German **Jews.** Most representatives refused to raise their country's quota.

Some said harsh, **anti-Semitic** things. Australia's representative said: "We don't have a racial problem—and we don't want one." Canada's said: "None is too many," meaning they did not want to take in any Jewish refugees. The Netherlands and Denmark were the only European countries to raise their quotas slightly.

Some Who Helped

Many individuals, both Christians and Jews, all over the world, worked hard to bring in as many refugees as possible. Various committees, such as the U.S. Committee for the Protection of European Children, raised money, found homes, and did what they could to help. There were Jewish communities in most parts of the world who worked to get refugees out of Germany and settled in new homes. All of these groups would have found their work much easier with government support.

Open Mockery

By February 1939, when this photo was taken, blatant anti-Semitism was common in Germany. These actors are mocking Jews and Jewish ceremonies. The float in the background has a model of a burning synagogue on it.

CANADA
6,000

U.S.
102,200

VENEZUELA
600

BOLIVIA
7,000

BRAZIL
8,000

CHILE
14,000

URUGUAY
2,200

ARGENTINA
63,500

NORWAY
2,000

SWEDEN
3,000

NETHERLANDS
30,000

GREAT BRITAIN
52,000

DENMARK
3,000

BELGIUM
12,000

HUNGARY
3,000

FRANCE
30,000

YUGOSLAVIA
7,000

PORTUGAL
10,000

SPAIN
3,000

ITALY
5,000

PALESTINE
33,400

SWITZERLAND
5,000

SOUTH AFRICA
26,100

JAPAN
300

SHANGHAI,
CHINA 20,000

PHILIPPINES
700

AUSTRALIA
3,500

Scattering Worldwide

This map shows where German Jews went from 1933 to the end of 1938.

The United States had helped German refugees at first. It had not increased its quota of people allowed in from Germany, but it gave out visas for several years in advance. Thus, people could go to the U.S. in 1938 if they had a visa for 1940. By 1939 though, all of the visas for Germany for 1939, 1940, and 1941 had been given out. To go on giving visas in advance would be like having no quotas at all. So the U.S. embassies in Germany were told that refugees on the 1942 quota could not enter the U.S. until that date. People were desperate to leave, but their chances of leaving were shrinking. The number of Jewish people committing suicide rose rapidly. The only place in the world Jewish refugees could go without a visa was Shanghai in China—a one-way ticket allowed anyone to live there. The Jewish community already in Shanghai had to cope with huge numbers of refugees, most of them arriving penniless.

The **Nazis** also sent ships full of refugees to Shanghai. They forced Jews to board and charged them for tickets. While the poor were forced into Shanghai, the rich tried other methods. Georg Landauer, Director of the Central Bureau for the Settlement of German Jews in Palestine, said that in 1939:

Travel agencies, mainly in Paris, get in touch with embassies that can be bribed—mainly Central and Southern American republics—and buy visas at high prices. They then charge a high fee for getting these expensive visas.

Once war broke out in Europe on September 3, 1939, getting out of Germany became even harder still. Meanwhile, as Germany began to take over other countries in Europe, Jewish people in these countries came under Nazi control again.

Frank Foley

Bribery was not the only way to bend the rules. Frank Foley, the Berlin-based British Passport Controller for emigration to Palestine, helped many people get away. The British controlled Palestine and set quotas in 1936. Foley said:

> *We wish we could help as many people as we once did; we could get thousands out, not hundreds. Conditions are getting worse here for the **Jews**. I dread to think how they will suffer in the coming winter. They have no money, few ways of earning any, and there is very little housing. The quota is a calamity.*

How Did Foley Help?

Foley did as much as he could. He accepted obviously false guarantees of money (needed to get into Palestine) and granted more visas than he was supposed to. When he could not get people to Palestine, he also helped them to get fake visas to South American countries. If all else failed, he knew a number of escape routes in Europe that they could use, although this was the most dangerous way to try to get out. Foley left Berlin in late August 1939. Hubert Pollack, a Jewish lawyer who worked with Foley, and who Foley helped to leave in 1939, said:

> *The number of Jews saved from Germany would have been tens of thousands less, yes, tens of thousands less, if another official had sat in Foley's place and applied the rules strictly.*

Leaving Germany

This diagram shows the number of Jews leaving Germany from 1933 to 1945.

These official figures do not include the people who left by escape routes.

After war broke out in September 1939, borders were closed—even **Aryans** had difficulty leaving the country.

Year	Number leaving
1933	38,000
1934	22,000
1935	21,000
1936	24,500
1937	23,500
1938	40,000
1939	78,000
1940	15,000
1941	8,000
1942	None
1943	500
1944	None
1945	None

The Spanier Twins

Thirteen-year-old twins, Renee and Ines Spanier, were on the *St. Louis*. They and their parents found a home in the Netherlands. They were rounded up when the **Nazis** took over and were sent to Westerbork, a Dutch **transit camp** where Jews were kept until they could be sent to Auschwitz-Birkenau to be killed. Luckily, Dr. Spanier became the chief medical officer at the Westerbork hospital and the family was never sent to Auschwitz. After the war, the girls emigrated to the U.S. Dr. Spanier helped the survivors of Belsen camp, and then went back to live in Germany.

Sailing to Safety?

On May 13, 1939, a group of 930 **refugees** set off from Hamburg, Germany, to sail to the United States on the liner *St. Louis*. Of these, 734 had U.S. visas for 1942. Once they reached the Caribbean, they tried to find countries to take them in until 1942. Almost all of the South American countries refused. Only Cuba said it would take 24, no more. It even refused to take the relatives of people already living in Cuba, once it had reached 24. The ship sailed on to anchor off Miami on the coast of Florida. The refugees sent a personal message to the President of the United States, Franklin D. Roosevelt, asking permission to enter. He refused because they had no visas. The *St. Louis* had to return to Europe.

When the *St. Louis* reached Antwerp, Belgium, the refugees were a big news story. Journalists and photographers met them when they docked. The refugees made more appeals for countries to take them in.

Safe at Last?

All of the remaining passengers found homes outside Germany. Britain took 287 refugees. France, Belgium, and the Netherlands took the remaining 619. As Germany took over more and more of Europe, though, the refugees from the *St. Louis* were back under Nazi control. By the end of the war, about 600 of the refugees who had been forced to return to Europe were dead—murdered in the **Holocaust.**

Kristallnacht

Kristallnacht means "The Night of Broken Glass." It took place on November 9, 1938, when the **Nazis** organized an attack on synagogues and **Jewish** businesses and homes all over Germany.

The Official Motive

The Nazis said *Kristallnacht* was a response to the murder of a Nazi official in Paris by a young Jew on November 7. Herschel Grynszpan shot a Nazi official from the German embassy in Paris. They said he did this because his parents were in a group of several hundred Polish Jews living in Germany who had been rounded up, taken to the Polish border, and dumped there. As news of the Nazi official's murder spread the next day, there was some violence against Jews in especially **anti-Semitic** parts of Germany, such as Hesse. The Nazis encouraged the violence, while saying they were only involved in it to try to stop it.

Careful Planning

In fact, official Nazi documents show that *Kristallnacht* was carefully planned as a countrywide action. The Nazis had just been waiting for an incident to use as an excuse for the attacks. Overnight about 200 synagogues were destroyed across Germany and, according to an official Nazi report, most Jewish homes and businesses were damaged, if not destroyed. This level of destruction in such a short time could only have been possible with advance planning. The **Gestapo** in each area had already been told:

> *As many Jews as possible, especially rich ones, must be arrested. For the time being it should only be healthy men, not too old. As soon as they have been arrested, they should be sent to the nearest **concentration camp** as soon as possible.*

Kristallnacht in Mosbach

The contents of a synagogue in Mosbach burns on November 9, 1938. Many people who describe *Kristallnacht* say that the Torah and other sacred things were destroyed by the **SA, Hitler Youth,** and ordinary people.

Map labels:
- Hamburg *Alexander Gordon*
- Berlin *Anne Fox*
- THE NETHERLANDS
- GERMANY
- POLAND
- BELGIUM
- Leipzig
- Mosbach *Torah burned*
- Furth *Lorraine Allard*
- CZECHOSLOVAKIA
- FRANCE
- Regensburg
- AUSTRIA

All Over Germany

Kristallnacht attacks took place all over Germany. This map shows the location of events mentioned in the text.

Kristallnacht Across Germany

Anne Fox was a twelve-year-old Jewish girl, living with her parents in Berlin:

> It began with loud banging and the sound of broken glass. Downstairs the Nazis smashed the printing machines in the corner store. My parents locked and bolted our heavy front door. Two sisters from a shop across the street came to us in their nightclothes, terrified.

Lorraine Allard was fourteen and living with her parents in Furth, Bavaria. She had already experienced a lot of anti-Semitic abuse, but *Kristallnacht* was still a shock:

> I was woken at two in the morning by a terrible banging on the door. Two uniformed Nazis were shouting "You're all under arrest! Dress and come with us." We were herded to a big square. There were thousands of other Jews, thousands. They were beating up the rabbi. They had fetched the Torahs out of the synagogue and I think they were trampling on them. We were taken to a theater and made to watch while they made man after man jump over chairs and whipped them when they fell. All men under the age of sixty were then taken off to Dachau concentration camp.

Alexander Gordon, aged sixteen, was living in a Jewish orphanage in Hamburg:

> At 11 P.M. bullets were shot through the windows, there was all kinds of noise. We all went into the fields behind our building and hid between the rows of asparagus. Twenty of us sat there all night in the cold, we didn't know what to do. When one of us called the police, they just laughed. At dawn we went back to the house. The windows were smashed and everything was messed up. One of the attackers had waited for us. He said "Make sure you're all gone by this afternoon. Out! If not, can you see that tree? We'll hang you all on it."

25

Nazi Reactions to *Kristallnacht*

The **Nazis** saw *Kristallnacht* as a great success. Joseph Goebbels, in charge of Nazi **propaganda,** wrote in his diary:

> *From all over the **Reich** information is flooding in: 50, 70 synagogues are burning. The **Führer** has ordered that 20–30,000 **Jews** be arrested. Now popular anger rages. It should be allowed to go on.*

More than 260 synagogues were destroyed. Many more were damaged. Jewish homes and businesses were looted. Some people were forced out of their homes so non-Jewish people could live in them. The **Gestapo** arrested 20,000 Jews and took them to Dachau, Buchenwald, and Sachsenhausen **concentration camps.** The Nazis also set a special tax on Jews for repairs—a billion marks (close to $500,000). Of course, the money was not used to repair Jewish property.

Other Reactions to *Kristallnacht*

Non-Jewish Germans reacted in various ways. Some of them were overjoyed. Carlton Greene, a British journalist in Berlin, wrote home to the *Daily Telegraph*:

> ***Racial** hatred and hysteria seemed to take hold of otherwise perfectly decent people. Respectable mothers held up their babies to see the "fun." Non-Jewish women who told children off for looting Jewish toyshops were spat on and attacked by the mob as Jew-lovers.*

Not everyone was delighted by *Kristallnacht*. Bernt Englemann, who lived in Berlin, tried to stop the looting of Jewish homes in his apartment block. He remembers the next morning:

> *We went downstairs. The landlady was already there. A carpenter was replacing the door. My mother asked him to look and see if there was anything else he could mend. "Sure," he replied. "I've already looked—it's a mess in there. What a disgrace. It makes you ashamed to be German." The landlady and my mother worked for over an hour, sweeping up the broken glass and splintered wood. Other women in the building joined in.*

The Next Morning

These Jewish shopkeepers are cleaning up after *Kristallnacht* on the morning of November 10, 1938.

Jewish Reactions to *Kristallnacht*

Jewish people were shaken by *Kristallnacht*. They were especially shaken by the involvement of neighbors in the destruction and looting. It was no longer possible to believe that the Nazis were only going to persecute big business Jews.

It was also much harder for Jews to believe that neighbors would help and protect them from trouble. Norbert Wollheim remembers the crowd that watched his local synagogue in Berlin burning:

The people standing with me in front of the burning synagogues may have felt ashamed, but they didn't dare say so. The Nazis had made it clear: they had concentration camps for people who spoke against them. There were some who made nasty remarks. They were glad it had happened. They said the Jews had got what they deserved. That really shocked me.

After *Kristallnacht* many German Jews decided to leave, even if it meant leaving most of their possessions, and even some members of their family, behind.

Herr Kahn, arrested during *Kristallnacht*, was taken to Buchenwald camp. Once released, he left Germany as soon as he could, using a local escape network. Camp conditions were appalling:

*There were about 6,000 of us crowded into one barrack with no floor, just damp clay. We had plank beds, no mattresses, no blankets, no light. On the fourth day we were put into barracks with a bit more room. Those with money could buy food, eating utensils, clothes, medicine. We did not work, but had roll call morning and night, often lasting several hours. Many died just standing there. On the twentieth day I was one of about 300 to be released. We were shaved and our hair cut. An **SS** officer told us he hoped we had been rehabilitated and to prove it we should contribute to the **Winter Aid** charity. Then we had to pay for "tickets" home; no one could leave until all had tickets. We were warned not to talk about our experiences, or we would be brought back and never get out alive. "Processing" took all day, with no food.*

Hating Jews

One of the most important steps in the **Nazis'** persecution and destruction of the **Jewish** people was to stop other people from seeing Jews as human beings. In the 1920s, they had started producing a stream of **anti-Semitic propaganda.** They always talked about "the Jew," which had a strange effect on many Germans. Non-Jewish Germans often believed anti-Semitic propaganda, even though they had Jewish friends and family. Bruno Hahnel was in the **SA** and said in a television interview in the 1990s:

> *I had Jewish relatives. I was very close to two Jewish cousins, but this didn't stop me agreeing with anti-Jewish Party ideas and actions.*

"The Jew"

Nazi propaganda concentrated on making people hate the Nazi version of Jewish people: "the Jew." This imaginary person was working constantly against Germany and its people. Melita Maschmann was in the **Hitler Youth** and clearly remembers how the Nazis helped to make real Jewish people less human:

> *We were brought up to see "the Jews" as wicked. When I said in meetings that Jews were the cause of all the misery of the world, or that Jewish blood was corrupting, I did not have to think of old Herr Lewy or Rosel Cohen, real people I knew: I thought only of the bogeyman "the Jew." And when I heard that "the Jews" were being driven from their professions and homes and imprisoned in **ghettos,** I automatically thought around the fact that this could happen to old Lewy, too. It was only "the Jew" who was being persecuted and made harmless.*

GROSSE POLITISCHE SCHAU IM BIBLIOTHEKSBAU DES DEUTSCHEN MUSEUMS

Anti-Semitic Propaganda

This poster is advertising the anti-Semitic film, *The Eternal Jew.* The man on the poster is the Nazi stereotype of a Jew: a dark, heavy-featured moneylender, making a profit out of "good Germans." The Nazis showed Jews as harsh employers (symbolized by the whip) who worked with the **Communists** (the Soviet Union is represented by a hammer and a sickle under the man's arm). The Nazis expected the German people to hate "the Jew" and many people did, without thinking clearly about it.

Isolation

The next step in Nazi persecution was to cut Jewish people off from everyone else. The less contact that people had with Jewish people, the less likely they were to see them as real people. Thus, Germans would be more likely to accept Nazi propaganda. Also, Nazi persecution of the Jews would be easier to ignore. The Nazis decided to cut Jewish people off by forcing them into ghettos in Poland, which Germany had taken over in September 1939. Security Police Special Units were told to set up ghettos as a temporary solution to the "Jewish Problem." These ghettos were set up in Polish cities that had good railroad connections. The Special Units were told: "Jewish congregations of over 500 members will be dissolved and moved to the ghettos."

Ghettos were set up in the most run-down areas of the cities. They often had limited water and electricity supplies and were crowded. It was not unusual for more than one family to live in one room.

The Nazis then filmed the ghettos, showing the Jews as dirty and uncivilized—having made sure they had no choice but to appear this way. A Nazi official visited Warsaw and wrote:

> *If there are any people left who still sympathize with the Jews they should come and look at a ghetto. Seeing the **race** lumped together, decaying and rotten to the core, will get rid of any sentiment.*

The Power of Language

The Nazis used language to make the Jews seem less than human. They used words such as "sub-human," "vermin," "filth," "vile polluters," "corrupters," "lepers," and "a plague"—never "people"—to refer to Jews. By the time they came to kill Jewish people in large numbers, they were calling them "cargo" or *stuecke*—which means "pieces," and was usually used to talk about things made in factories.

Real Life

This is a photo of two Jewish children at a summer camp in Sweden in the early 1900s. If you compare them to the Nazi propaganda about "the Jew" and the poster on page 28, you can see how they failed to fit Nazi ideas at all. They are fair, healthy, clean, and well dressed. They are clearly not a threat to anyone. They are just ordinary children.

Did the German Churches Help the Jews?

How did the various churches in Germany react to the **Nazi** persecution of the **Jews?** Many of the established Christian churches were happy to see a strong Nazi government that provided jobs and welfare for the poor and that was against **Communism** (which the churches also opposed). Church organizations did not openly criticize the way the Nazis treated Jews. However, there were a number of church members who bravely criticized Nazi **anti-Semitism.** They were sent to **concentration camps** or executed.

The Catholic Church

The German Catholic Church did not protest against Nazi anti-Semitism. In 1933, it made an agreement with Hitler that he would not attack the Church if it did not get involved in politics. So, the German Catholic Church did not speak out against Nazi anti-Semitic policies; it even let the Nazis use its records to determine if people were "Jewish."

Catholic groups in countries not controlled by the Nazis, such as Britain and the United States, protested and set up organizations to help **refugees,** especially "non-**Aryan** Christians." This group included people with Jewish **ancestors** who had converted to Christianity, but were classified by the Nazis as Jewish.

Some Catholics condemned the Nazis; others supported them. Emma Becker was a German Jew who married a Catholic and converted to Catholicism. Despite this, the Catholics at her church would not sit or kneel beside her or let her sing in the church choir. Only the priest accepted her, so his congregation turned against him, too. When a Catholic priest, Bernhard Lichtenberg of Berlin, asked his congregation to pray for "the poor, persecuted Jews," he was arrested and sent to Dachau concentration camp where he died.

The Protestant Churches

There was no single Protestant church, but several different Protestant movements that did not always agree. These churches reacted to the Nazis differently. The German Christian Movement accepted Nazi beliefs, including anti-Semitism. The Nazis gave this church more support than any other because its members were happy to hang Nazi swastikas in their churches and to preach Nazi ideas. However, there were too many Protestant churches for the Nazis to control them all.

A new group, the Confessing Church, was set up to oppose the German Christian Movement and its "political" behavior. They were persecuted by the **Gestapo,** and many members were sent to concentration camps.

Ways of Resisting

As with the German Catholic Church, it was most often individual people, rather than whole organizations, that spoke out against the Nazis. Pastor Martin Niemoeller was arrested on July 1, 1937, after a sermon in which he said: "No more are we ready to keep silent at man's command when God commands us to speak. We must obey God rather than man."

Some Protestant churches opposed the Nazis more openly, especially when their governments were doing so, too. The churches in Nazi-**occupied** Denmark and Norway, for example, protested against the **deportation** of their Jewish populations by the Nazis. The Bulgarian Church joined the rest of the country in direct action to save their Jewish population. **Jehovah's Witnesses,** who refused to say *"Heil Hitler"* and would not serve in the army, were banned from state after state in Germany starting in 1933. They were treated as a political threat and put in concentration camps. Other Christian groups, like the **Quakers,** worked secretly to help Jews escape. They did not speak out openly against the Nazis, but worked to save as many lives as possible while seeming to be "good Germans."

Using Religion

While Hitler was certainly anti-Christian, he and the Nazis were willing to use religion to get people fighting. This army belt buckle bears the slogan, "God is with us."

Benefiting from Nazi Policies

Different Germans reacted in different ways to the **Nazi's** treatment of the **Jews.** Many did not dare to argue with the Nazis, for fear of the **concentration camps.** Others took advantage of the fact that, under Nazi law, Jewish people lost their jobs and businesses, and they took these over for themselves. Others went further, taking advantage of the fact that people could persecute Jews and get away with it. They could steal from Jews, beat them up, even kill them, and the **Gestapo** would not care. A young doctor remembers happily accepting Nazi policies in 1933:

> I wasn't much interested in politics. But I wondered if Hitler coming to power might be good for me. So many people were complaining that Germany had too many doctors. With Hitler in power he would "eliminate" the Jewish competition, so we **"Aryans"** could have a profitable practice. Please, don't misunderstand! At home we had Jewish neighbors we got on well with; our family doctor was Jewish. I wasn't **prejudiced!**

Businessmen

From 1937 on, the Nazis "Aryanized" Jewish businesses by taking them from their owners and giving them to Aryan businessmen. Sometimes a small amount was paid for the business, but never what it was worth. Many people were quick to take advantage of these "sales." Others reacted against them. One Nazi party member and member of the **SA** had been given the job of organizing "Aryanization" in Munich. He resigned, saying that while he was a good Party member and admirer of Hitler:

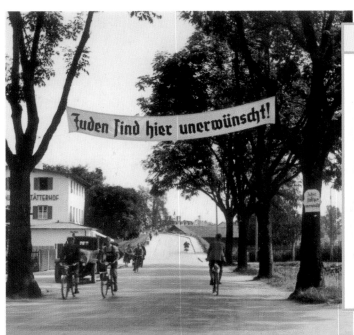

Jew Free

Many towns, such as the Austrian one in this picture, threw out all of their Jewish residents, making the town **Judenfrei—** "Jew Free." They then put up banners saying "Jews not welcome here" (as in the photo) or "This town is Jew free." Some places even changed their road signs to show their **anti-Semitism.** One such sign said: "Careful! Sharp bend! Slow! Jews—75 miles an hour!" As towns were "cleansed" of Jews, local people who were not Jewish took over Jewish-owned homes and businesses.

I can no longer stand by and accept the way many "Aryan" businessmen are grabbing Jewish shops and factories at ridiculous prices. They are like vultures swarming down to feed on the Jewish carcass.

One Example of Greed

Kurt Fuchel, who later escaped to Britain, remembers the day after *Kristallnacht* in Vienna:

A woman had tried to buy our flat [apartment], *but my parents had refused to sell. She came round the morning after* Kristallnacht *and said "It's mine now, don't argue or I'll have you sent to a concentration camp." She showed us a piece of paper with a swastika stamped on it. We had to leave. The woman had gone to the local government offices and had been given a document that gave her ownership of the flat* [apartment].

War!

On September 1, 1939, Hitler began World War II with an invasion of Poland. The war was decisive for the **Holocaust** against Europe's Jews. Prior to the war, Hitler was only able to persecute German Jews—a relatively small number. As Nazi victories allowed him to occupy most of Europe, however, the number of potential victims of the Nazis rose into the millions.

33

Legitimized Killing

In March 1938, Germany had taken over Austria. Hitler said he was only putting right the unfair Treaty of Versailles that had taken land from Germany, but Austria had never been part of Germany. Then, in October 1938, Hitler, with British and French consent, took over the German-speaking part of Czechoslovakia (Sudetenland). On March 9, 1939, he invaded the rest of Czechoslovakia. Hitler had waited to see if the other European countries would go to war over Czechoslovakia. They did not. So, on September 1, 1939, Hitler's army invaded Poland. Britain and France then declared war on Germany on September 3. It was too late, though. The German army was too strong. It swept across Poland with stunning speed. Germany and the Soviet Union, had made an agreement in 1939 not to fight each other. They also had decided how to divide up Poland, and so Poland was split up. Germany wanted the agreement because it did not want to have to fight the Soviet Union as well as Britain and France. The Soviet Union wanted the agreement because its army was not yet strong enough to take on the German army.

borders in 1933	
---- extent of German occupation	
Germany in 1933	
Germany by end of 1938	
Germany by end of 1939	
Germany by end of 1940	
Germany by end of 1941	
Countries controlled by or allied to Germany by end of 1941	

German Expansion

This map shows how **Nazi** Germany took over more and more of Europe from 1933 to 1945. As the Nazis controlled more territory, more **Jewish** people were caught up in the **Holocaust.** In the early 1930s, many Jews left Germany for the safety of France, the Netherlands, or Belgium, only to find these countries taken over by Germany during the war.

Mass Graves

Here is an *Einsatzgruppen* in action. Their system was to dig a mass grave and assemble all of the Jews in one place, such as the town square. The Jews were then taken in batches, men first, and then women and children. Everyone had to strip. Then they were shot on the edge of the mass grave, so that their bodies would fall in.

Not Just Fighting

The war changed Nazi tactics toward non-**Aryans,** especially Jews. Hitler did not need to worry about what other countries thought of his actions anymore—he was already at war. Also, people get killed in war, so it is easier to blur the line between people who are enemies and people who are "garbage," as the Nazis put it. So the army that marched into Poland did not merely pass laws against Jews and Poles (Poles were Slavs and thus "sub-human" to the Nazis). It killed them, too— thousands of them. It was in Poland that the Nazis set up many **concentration camps,** the biggest **ghettos, labor camps,** and the only **death camps.**

Mass Murder

During the very first days of the war, Private Georg Neuber, a soldier in the German army, witnessed the cruelty of German **SS** and special operations units toward the Polish people. Near Naklo, his company saw about 80 Jews murdered. In a village near Bromberg, they found the bodies of over 50 Poles in a schoolhouse.

Not one seemed to be over twenty; all had been shot in the neck. Soldiers from his company were not made to take part in the mass executions, but in the following weeks they watched many more. Time and again, Jewish men, women, and children were hauled away and "liquidated," allegedly for shooting at Nazis. The same fate befell many Poles.

On June 22, 1941, the Germans invaded the Soviet Union, despite the Nazi-Soviet Pact. The Soviets were both **Communists** and Slavs—two reasons for Hitler to hate them. The invasion of Poland had been brutal. The invasion of the Soviet Union was worse. The Nazis set up special murder squads, called *Einsatzgruppen,* that moved with the invading army. Their official orders were to murder **partisans—** local people who resisted the German **occupation.** It soon became clear that their real purpose was to kill all Jews. The *Einsatzgruppen* used local people to pick out the Jews. These people were rewarded with their choice of the property of the dead.

Hiding the Truth

The **Nazis** were killing **Jews** in large numbers, but they were still not openly saying so. They were supposedly "executing **partisans**." However, they were admitting to themselves that they now wanted to make German lands *Judenfrei* through murder, although they seldom talked of "murdering Jews." Instead, even in official reports, they talked about soldiers in the Soviet Union "making sure the Jewish sub-humans pay a severe, but fair, price for their misdeeds." When they talked of bad conditions in labor gangs and camps, they said these would "naturally reduce Jewish numbers."

Too Upsetting?

The *Einsatzgruppen* killed thousands of Jews in the Soviet Union—in Babi Yar near Kiev, 33,000 people were murdered in two days. The head of the **SS**, Heinrich Himmler, was worried about the effect of this work on his squads. Himmler wanted less personal ways of killing:

> *For shootings, you need people to do the shooting, and it has a bad effect on them. It would be better to liquidate people using "gas-vans" which have been made to my design in Germany. They remove the unpleasantness connected with execution by shooting.*

Recording a Massacre

On September 14, 1941, the *Einsatzgruppen* killed 2,000 Jews in Dubossary in the Soviet Union. Some squads had several soldiers firing into the mass grave. It was thought to be "less upsetting" than individual shootings, in which a soldier knew exactly who he had killed.

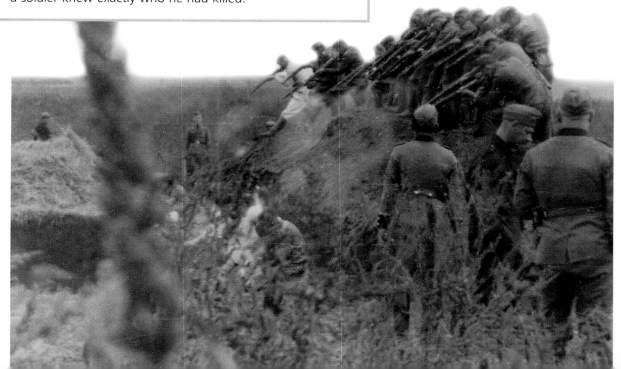

Gassing in Auschwitz

On September 3, 1941, about 600 Soviet prisoners of war and 250 patients from the camp hospital were driven into a sealed cellar. They were gassed with Zyklon B gas, which the camp had supplies of because it was used for killing lice on clothing and bedding. Although personnel did have to make the prisoners go into the cellar and did have to throw the can of gas in, they killed a lot of people at one time, without having to hear them die. Thousands of cans of Zyklon B, as shown in this picture, were found at Auschwitz when the war ended.

Gas Vans

The SS, looking for less "unpleasant" ways of mass murder, settled on gassing as the best method. At first they tried "gas vans," vans that pumped exhaust fumes into the back where the victims were, while the van was driven around. The designers experimented to get the vans working efficiently. One report said:

> *The vans must be smaller and packed solid to shorten the operating time. The makers said this would put too much weight at the front. It does not, because the "goods" [the people inside] rush to the rear and are mostly there at the end of the operation.*

In July 1941, Hermann Goering, Hitler's second-in-command, told Himmler that Hitler had decided that the "Final Solution" to the Jewish problem was to kill them all. While the *Einsatzgruppen* were doing this in Russia, Himmler was to look for places for **death camps.** They had to be in Poland and isolated—with a railway line nearby. He also had to find an efficient and impersonal way to commit mass murder.

The Chelmno Gas Vans

Chelmno camp—the first death camp—was set up in December 1941. It is where Himmler's gas-van experiments took place. The vans pumped carbon monoxide exhaust fumes into the sealed rear compartment. SS scientists found that a ten-mile (sixteen-kilometer) drive from the "load point" to the burial trenches, at a speed of 20 mph (32 kph), was long enough to kill the "goods." The gas vans were still too personal, however. The drivers often drove faster than 20 mph (32 kph), to get the job done quickly, but then the Jews were not dead on arrival. Thus, the drivers had to drive around for longer, or the officers in charge had to shoot the dying people.

The "Final Solution"

On January 20, 1942, the **Nazis** staged a conference in Wannsee, just outside of Berlin. Reinhard Heydrich, head of the German security operations, called the meeting. The purpose was to plan the outline of the "Final Solution" and to establish the authority of the **SS** in carrying it out. "There are about 3.5 million Jews in my territory," said Hans Frank, the Nazi Governor-General of **Occupied** Poland. "We cannot shoot them all, we cannot poison them all. We have to find ways to wipe them all out."

The Nazis left the conference with two different aims. They wanted to kill all of the Jews in the land they controlled. They also wanted more soldiers, so they had to make workers join the army.

Workers who joined the army had to be replaced. **Concentration camp** prisoners could be worked hard and not paid. Meanwhile, the Nazis set up **death camps** to "deal with" Jews. Death camps were mainly separate from the concentration camps and **labor camps** that provided workers. Auschwitz-Birkenau and Majdanek were exceptions; they were both concentration and death camps.

Ready for Mass Murder

Jews from the **ghettos,** the camps, and occupied Europe were taken to the death camps. Jews left alive were simply waiting their turn. Belzec, Chelmno, Treblinka, and Sobibor death camps were built. In the death camps, Jews were gassed in large numbers. From 1942, the SS in the camps and ghettos treated Jews even worse than before. They were worked to death, starved to death, beaten to death, and shot.

Ways of Killing

These Jewish people are being **transported** to Chelmno death camp. They were told they were going to a different ghetto. While the death camps were working, Jews were still killed at random in the concentration camps and ghettos. Harry Balsam was twelve years old in 1942, living in the Polish ghetto of Gorlice. "Killing and shooting became a normal, everyday event," he remembers. "That is how it was. You got used to the idea that killing was nothing."

Death Camps

The death camps killed millions of Jews in a few years. Treblinka camp gassed people for a year and a week—53 weeks. In that time, it killed 700,000 people; that is 2,000 people a day, seven days a week. By 1942, the Nazis had made Jews seem so unlike human beings that some people gave little or no thought to killing them. Random violence against Jews from 1933 on, followed by more killings on a larger and larger scale, made killing Jews seem normal. The death camps ran a system that deliberately made the victims as unlike people as possible. This system helped the SS who ran the camps to cope with their duty. In 1971, Hungarian journalist Gitta Sereny interviewed Franz Stangl, the camp commandant of Treblinka, in Dusseldorf (Germany) prison. During the interview, it became clear that once the victims had undressed they had no longer been real to him.

Numbers of Dead

This map shows the approximate number of Jews murdered and the countries they came from.

A Different Way of Looking

The following is part of Gitta Sereny's interview with Franz Stangl, commandant of Treblinka camp:

Gitta Sereny: *There were so many children—did they ever make you think of your children?*

Franz Stangl: *No, I can't say I ever thought that way. You see, I rarely saw them as individuals. It was always a huge mass. I sometimes stood on a wall and saw them in the "tube"* [the fenced path to the gas chambers]. *But—how can I explain it— they were naked, packed together, running, being driven with whips like . . .* [The sentence trailed off.]

Gitta: *Could you not have changed that? You were in charge. Could you not have stopped the nakedness, the whips, the horror of treating them like cattle?*

Franz: *No, no, no. This was the system. It worked. And because it worked, it could not be changed.*

Gitta: *What was the worst place in the camp for you?*

Franz: *The undressing barrack.*

Reactions

How much did people in land **occupied** by the **Nazis** know about the **Holocaust?** How much did people in countries free from Nazi control know? There is much argument about this, even now. For a long time, "ordinary" Germans claimed that they had no idea what was going on in Nazi camps, especially the **death camps.** Certainly, the Nazis did not publicize the death camps. This does not mean that people had no idea what was happening.

People must have seen the **concentration** and **labor camps**—many of them were based in or near cities. Daniel Jonah Goldhagen, author of *Hitler's Willing Executioners*, points out:

> *Within Germany itself there was an enormous network of camps—it is not certain how many. If you count in the smallest sub-camps, Berlin had 645 camps just for forced labor.*

Making Excuses?

Even today, there are people who want to excuse not only ordinary Germans, but also the **SS** and the ***Einsatzgruppen.*** One of the lawyers prosecuting people involved in the Holocaust said:

> *So many people tell me they are "sick and tired about hearing lies about our soldiers," that the people we investigate "didn't know what they were doing" or "were just obeying orders." They knew. One hundred and thirty-two SS men in the Soviet Union killed 138,000 men, women, and children in seven months by shooting each one in the back of the neck. They kept careful lists. How could they not know what they were doing?*

Far From Invisible

During the war, concentration camp prisoners were used to clear the streets after British bombing raids. These prisoners are working in Bremen, Germany, after the bombing raid of June 13, 1943. The Nazis were careful to choose prisoners who looked as healthy as possible, and they made sure they were reasonably dressed. In this way, they made camp conditions seem better than they were for many prisoners, especially **Jewish** prisoners.

Help at Last

Rudolf Vrba (right) and Alfred Wetzler escaped as the SS at Birkenau prepared to gas all of the Hungarian Jews. Vrba remembers that it was clear what was going on:

> They were talking about "a million units," even "Hungarian salami." This had some effect—the British bombed the rail lines to Auschwitz, while the U.S.A. bombed Budapest, Hungary's capital city. The Hungarian government stopped sending Jews to Auschwitz.

The escapees' information saved over 170,000 people.

MINISTERSTVO NÁRODNEJ OBRANY

Čj. 15550/34/Vr-50 Kleg. 5. oddel. 1946

Vlastnoručný podpis majiteľa

We will never know how much "ordinary people" knew and how much they chose to ignore. Some Germans refused to see the problems with Nazi rule. Many others lost their first enthusiasm for the Nazis, but felt powerless to change things. Grete Kulle, who lived in Berlin, remembers:

> My mother meant it when she said: "The riffraff have to be cleared off the streets. They will be re-educated to do honest work in the camps. They will be taught discipline and cleanliness, but will not be harmed." But you could not claim that you had no idea what was going on, not if you read the paper. People would say "Hush! Watch Out! You don't want to end up in a concentration camp!"

Tomi Ungerer says the same thing about life in **occupied** France: "The word 'concentration camp' was used in posters as a threat. Stories went around that the wartime soap was made from Jewish victims."

What About Other Countries?

From 1933 on, it was clear to people outside Germany that concentration camps were harsh, especially on Jews. During the war, the British heard of Birkenau almost from the very beginning. In October 1943, there were even newspaper headlines such as "Hitler Murdered Three Million Jews in Europe." The British and U.S. governments were focused on winning the war, though. Then, in 1944, Rudolf Vrba and Alfred Wetzler escaped from Auschwitz and told what was happening in Birkenau. Their report was widely publicized. It was no longer possible to ignore the facts.

Collaboration

At the end of the war, many countries and people were accused of collaborating with the **Nazis.** They were said to have helped and worked with the Nazis. Some had collaborated willingly, because they agreed with Nazi ideas or benefited in some way. Others were forced to collaborate because of threats to themselves or their families.

Collaborating Countries

Countries collaborated with the Nazis in various ways. Hungary, Bulgaria, and Romania worked with the Nazis as **allies** in return for not being invaded by Germany. They still ran their own countries, but they had to follow Nazi policies. They collaborated by persecuting their **Jewish** residents. **Occupied** countries that were taken over by the Nazis collaborated in this way, too.

Did Everyone Collaborate?

It was possible to avoid collaborating, even if the German army was occupying your country. For example, the Danish hid Jews from Nazi officials who only managed to find 500 Jews to **transport.** In contrast, France sent 77,000 Jewish people to their deaths, most of them rounded up by the French police, not the **Gestapo** or **SS.**

Hungary sent transport after transport of Jews—about 437,000 people. On the other hand, as soon as the U.S. bombed Budapest, the Hungarian capital, and demanded that the transports stop, the Hungarian government did stop them. They refused to collaborate any more and 170,000 people were saved.

German Collaborators

People as well as countries collaborated with the Nazis. In Germany, people collaborated by reporting on and beating up **Communists** and Jews, throwing Jews out of their homes, and so on. Some of the information as to where Jews and Communists were came from ordinary people, but the Nazis had a spy system, too. In 1936, a Nazi official wrote to a friend:

> *Every staircase now has an informer who collects the **Winter Aid** contributions, gives out all sorts of forms, asks about family matters, and tries to find out about everything under the sun. He talks to housewives about prices and food shortages, he pushes into people's homes to see what newspapers they read, how they live, and so on. Even old Party members have protested about this snooping. Every tenant is visited at least once a week by one of these block wardens. They send in regular reports to their Party office.*

In occupied countries, people gave information to the Germans about Communists, Jews, political opponents, and **partisans**—people who secretly fought the Germans by blowing up bridges and railway lines or sabotaging the Nazis in other ways. Collaborators in occupied countries made a huge difference—if the local police and people did not help, then it was far harder for the Nazis to make lists of the Jews and act against them. Sometimes people were forced to collaborate. The Nazis were ruthless about threatening that people or their families would be sent to **concentration camps** if they did not help.

Punishing Collaborators

Once the Germans were driven out of France, many people who had collaborated with them were shot or hung by local partisans. People who had run cafés the Germans used, or women who had had relationships with German soldiers, were also seen as collaborators. While some people who were punished had certainly helped the Nazis and caused many deaths, others were killed in a settling of local rivalries. This photo was taken in Chartres, France, on August 18, 1944, shortly after the Allies drove the Germans out of the town. The women had their heads shaved because they had had relationships with German soldiers.

Getting the Children Out

The **Nazis** were very clear about the importance of children. They began to teach Nazi beliefs before children were even able to walk or talk, using nursery rhymes that praised Hitler, picture books, and so on. They also saw how important children were for the **races** they hated—children were the hope for the future. Wiping out the children of **Jews,** Poles, and Slavs became important. Other people thought it was important to save these children, for the same reason. Rabbi Joseph Cahaneman put it this way: "A child is an orphan when he has no parents. A nation is an orphan when it has no children."

When Jewish people trying to leave Germany could not get permission for everyone to leave, or visas for everyone to enter a country, they often sent their children first. It was a hard choice, but many people made it.

Organizations worked hard in Germany and Britain to make sure that many children got out in special groups known as *Kindertransports*. In September 1935, Albert and Paula Rabow were forced out of their home in Koenigsberg, Germany. They decided they had to get sixteen-year-old Miriam out. The waiting lists for Palestine were very long, so they traveled to Berlin to ask Frank Foley for help. He got Miriam out to Palestine in about a month.

Hedy Epstein's family tried to emigrate to the U.S. Their quota number came up before they had all the documents ready that they needed to leave Germany. They had to reregister and start again. They also tried to emigrate to Cuba and Lima, Peru. Finally, they got Hedy out on a *Kindertransport*. Her parents were sent to Auschwitz camp and died before the end of the war.

Identification Papers

The U.S. Embassy in Marseilles, France, gave this letter to a Jewish boy, Werner Goldsmidt. It meant he could go to the U.S. on the date arranged by the U.S. Committee for the Protection of European Children, despite the fact that the French government had not yet given him a passport. He was twelve when he left for the United States.

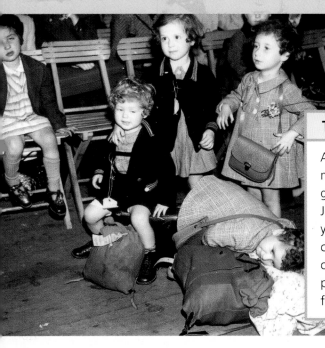

Smuggled Out of Germany

Before the war began, some Jewish children were smuggled out of Germany on student exchanges. The Nazis allowed "approved" students to go to places like Britain. Bernt Englemann, now a journalist, went on several exchanges. Before his second exchange, Herr Desch, a local tailor, seemingly a Nazi supporter, spoke to him:

> Herr Desch asked about my school exchange to England—who organized it, how many were going, what the route was, and how much attention the border guards paid to this regular group. When I caught the train, Herr Desch joined it with a party of sixteen children. When the exchange students for Liege in France left the train, Herr Desch's group did, too. One of the teachers told me they were going to the U.S.A.

By August 1939, Desch had gotten several hundred people out of Germany, most of them Jewish children. He gave them money and made sure they were safe with relatives or with his **Quaker** friends.

A Humane Official

Norbert Wollheim was 25 when he began to organize the *Kindertransports* from Berlin. He and the other supervising adults had to promise to return to Berlin or the *Kindertransports* would stop. He remembers one *Kindertransport* in particular:

> We were on the boat before we found that one boy was eighteen. I went to find him and saw his head was shaved— he'd been in a **concentration camp.** To send him back to Germany would be to send him to his death. We decided to say he was really seventeen. We landed at Harwich, dead tired, and I was called to the supervisor about the boy's age. I said he was seventeen in our records. We called the boy in to say when he was born (we'd made him learn the wrong year on the boat). He stuttered it out. The immigration officer looked at him shaking, with his shaven head. We were lying, and he knew we were lying, but he stamped "Admit" on the boy's papers and saved his life.

Settling In

The *Kindertransports* saved lives, but the children had very different experiences in Britain. Their experiences depended partly on their ages and partly on where they were sent to live. Some went to live with relatives. Some went to live with strangers, but settled in and had a fairly stable life throughout the war. Others could not settle and were moved from family to family. Most of the *kinder* left Germany expecting to see their parents again. Very few of them did.

Anne Fox

Anne Fox was born in Berlin in 1926. In 1933, her father had his job in a bank taken away and it took several months for him to find a poorly paid job in a **Jewish** company. As the situation for Jews in Berlin got worse, Anne's Uncle Walter,

who lived in London, managed to get Anne's brother, Günter, a student visa to England. After *Kristallnacht*, Günter found a family to support Anne in England. Anne's parents arranged for her to leave. Anne remembers:

> *The children met at the railway station, tagged and labeled, dragging rucksacks [backpacks], suitcases, dolls, stuffed animals, and musical instruments. Parents hid their grief as best they could. There were hugs and kisses, handkerchiefs waving from open windows.*

When Anne reached London, Günter took her to stay with their Uncle Walter. After about a week, Anne went to live with the Pincus family. Anne tried to fit in:

> *Mrs. Pincus was kind, but she was not my mother and her home was not our Berlin flat [apartment], either. I spoke some English, so was able to get on a bit at school. There was another German **refugee** in my class, called Mia. We talked German together, gossiped about our foster families, and laughed at the strange behavior of the British. We were a bit of a mystery to our classmates.*

How Old?

This photo shows some of the older *kinder* arriving in England in 1939. Parents tried to "fix" their children's ages to get them on a *Kindertransport*.

Blitz!

In the late summer of 1939, the British government drew up plans for children and pregnant women to be evacuated from British cities they thought the Germans would bomb when war broke out. On September 3, 1939, the evacuation began. Although the bombing did not begin at once, when it came, it was devastating. It was referred to as "the Blitz." This photo of a bombed London street was taken in 1940.

At War

The *kinder* arrived as Britain was preparing for war. This was especially noticeable for children, like Anne, living in London:

> *By the autumn the British were imposing a complete blackout routine. . . . In school, we were told to be ready for evacuation. Everyone was given a gas mask in a cardboard box and we had to take a rucksack [backpack] to school each day, in case we had to go.*

Anne and her school were evacuated out of London to Swineshead, a small village. Anne went to live with the Manfield family, where she was very happy. At this time, she was still getting letters from her parents. By the time she was nearly fifteen, Anne was too old for the village school.

Günter found Anne a place at Bunce Court, a Jewish-run boarding school. In February 1941, Anne left for Bunce Court, where there were many other *kinder*. While Anne was in Bunce Court, the letters from her parents stopped arriving. Günter had joined the army and, in 1942, he married a British girl.

In the summer of 1943, Anne left school and went to live with her sister-in-law, Constance, in Cardiff, Wales. She worked as a dressmaker's assistant and then at the local library. It was while she was working at the library, just after the war in Europe had ended, that she met an American soldier, Frank Fox. They became friends, eventually married, and moved to Philadelphia, Pennsylvania.

Kurt Fuchel

Kurt Fuchel was an only child, born in 1931. He and his parents were forced out of their apartment on *Kristallnacht* by an **Aryan** who wanted it. His parents could see that it was important to leave Germany as soon as possible and contacted the *Kindertransport* program to get Kurt out. Kurt was put on a ship to England and was taken in by a **Jewish** family. Percy and Miriam Cohen lived in Norwich, England, and had a son, John, who was five. Kurt remembers being met and taken to the Cohen's home:

I was scared, but they bathed me, gave me clean clothes, and we had a chicken dinner. I began to feel more at home. I was sent for English lessons, then to John's school, which was small and had kind teachers. At first, I cried for my parents, but Miriam comforted me.

Kurt remembers trying to fit in:

I really tried to please my foster parents. Suddenly having a brother was a shock, as an only child. I was jealous and would say to Miriam, "You don't love me as much as John." Then she would say, "I do." I was really worried, once I'd settled in, that I would be sent away. This happened quite a lot. One family took in a girl who was the same age as their daughter and the girls fought all the time—hair-pulling, screaming, fighting the lot. So she went. You would have thought us exiles would have got together a lot, spoke our language, talked about old times. But we avoided each other. I was terrified that if one of us did something wrong it would affect how people felt about the others.

Looking for Work

Lore Segal found it hard to settle in England and was moved around from family to family, because she didn't seem happy enough or grateful enough. She had a heavy burden to carry. Her parents had asked her to find people willing to hire them as employees and thus guarantee them work in Britain. Many *kinder*, despite their youth, were expected to do this, to get their parents out of Germany. People without anyone to search for them had to rely on advertisements like these. Lore eventually found work for her parents and got them out of Germany. They had to work as servants, though, and it ruined her father's health.

Together Again

This photo shows Kurt Fuchel (*far left*) with Deborah Oppenheimer in 2000 at the world premiere of *Into the Arms of Strangers*, the Oscar-winning documentary film that tells the story of English *kinder*.

The photo below, shows Kurt with his parents in Toulouse, France, in 1949. By the time it was taken, the family had been together for almost two years. While all three knew they were lucky to have survived, they still found it hard to get used to each other all over again after such a long time apart. The Cohens found the separation hard, too. Miriam remembers the day they handed Kurt over to his parents. "It was very, very sad. He didn't want to go. He didn't know them any more."

After the war in Europe was over, Kurt's parents got in touch with the Cohens. His parents had escaped to southern France, and some kind people hid them through the war. Kurt can remember how he felt when he heard the news:

I was told that I would have to go back to live with them. I think I was horrified by the idea. Uncle Percy persuaded them that I should finish my education in England until my exams when I was sixteen.

In 1947 the Cohens took me to Paris to meet my parents. I saw them coming towards me and I felt this really strong emotion—I was happy, I remembered loving them. We went out to eat and there were the Cohens on one side and my parents on the other and I couldn't really speak German or French, so it was hard to talk to them. They had let go of a seven-year-old and got back a sixteen-year-old. It was very hard for all of us. I was lucky, most kinder *never saw their parents again, but it was hard for all of us to adjust.*

Most of the children who escaped on the *Kindertransports* did not find their families again. After the war, they settled in

different parts of the world. They did not quite know how to discuss their experiences. It was hard to call themselves "survivors" when they had escaped Germany and the camps. Yet they had been torn away from their families and most of them had never seen their parents again. They had survived and they had to cope with feeling guilty about that, too. It was not until many years after the war that a member of the *Kindertransports* organized a reunion and the *kinder* talked about their experiences and shared their anger at being sent away, even to be safe.

Timeline

1933

January 30	Hitler comes to power in Germany as Chancellor.
February 27	A fire breaks out at the *Reichstag*, the German Parliament. The **Nazis** blame the **Communists** and produce a Dutch Communist who confesses.
February 28	German President Hindenburg's decree, "For the Protection of the People and the State," allows for the creation of **concentration camps.** The Nazis persuade Hindenburg to pass the decree to fight what they called the "Communist threat" after the fire at the *Reichstag*.
March 5	New elections are held. The Nazis win easily with intimidation.
April 1	**Jewish** stores in Berlin are boycotted.
April 7	Jewish government employees, including civil servants, teachers, and professors, lose their jobs.
April 24–25	People with Jewish names can no longer use them when sending telegrams. Jews are excluded from all sporting organizations.
May 10	Books written by Jews, "degenerates," liberals, and Nazi opponents are burned.
October	Jews are no longer allowed to work in the media.

1934

March 5	Jewish actors are banned.
June 7	Jewish students are banned from taking exams.

1935

September 15	The Nuremberg Laws are passed against German Jews.

1936

	Jewish doctors and dentists cannot work in state hospitals. Jews cannot become judges, join the army, or work in the book trade.

1937

	Jewish businesses are **"Aryanized."**

1938

March 13	Germany takes over Austria.
March 15	The German army marches into Prague, Czechoslovakia.
June 25	Jewish doctors can no longer treat non-Jewish patients.
September 30	Germany takes the Sudetenland as a result of the Munich Agreement.
November 9	Synagogues are burned and stores and homes are looted in *Kristallnacht*.

1939

March 15	Germany takes control of all of Czechoslovakia.
September 1	Germany invades Poland and takes immediate action against Polish Jews.
September 3	Britain and France declare war on Germany.
September 28	Germany and the Soviet Union split Poland up between them.

1940

April 9	Germany invades Denmark and Norway.
April 30	The Nazis set up the Lodz **Ghetto** in Poland.
May 10	Germany invades Belgium, France, Luxembourg, and Holland.

Places of Interest and Websites

Florida Holocaust Museum
55 Fifth Street South
St. Petersburg, FL 33701
Visitor information: (727) 820-0100
Website: *http://www.flholocaustmuseum.org*

Holocaust Memorial Center
6602 West Maple Road
West Bloomfield, MI 48322
Visitor information: (248) 661-0840
Website: *http://holocaustcenter.org*

Holocaust Museum Houston
5401 Caroline Street
Houston, TX 77004
Visitor information: (713) 942-8000
Website: *http://www.hmh.org*

Simon Wiesenthal Center: Museum of Tolerance
Simon Wiesenthal Plaza
9786 West Pico Blvd.
Los Angeles, CA 90035
Visitor information: (310) 553-8403
Website: *http://www.museumoftolerance.com*

United States Holocaust Memorial Museum
100 Raoul Wallenberg Place, SW
Washington, D.C. 20024
Visitor information: (202) 488-0400
Website: *http://www.ushmm.org*

Website warning
1. Almost all Holocaust websites have been designed for adult users. They may contain horrifying and upsetting information and pictures.
2. Some people wish to minimize the Holocaust, or even deny that it happened at all. Some of their websites pretend to be delivering unbiased facts and information. To be sure of getting accurate information, it is always best to use an officially recognized site such as the ones listed on this page.
3. If you plan to visit a Holocaust website, ask an adult to view the site with you.

Index